I0418737

"Caitlin Johnson's imaginative trip through realms both dark and beautiful is nothing short of captivating. This is quite the poetic study on our relationship with death, and it shows a signature defiance. Johnson says, "My body crackles in spite of death, / and I ask my soul to travel with it." That's exactly what this book is: a journey alongside death, littered with spellbinding imagery and elegant, if not useful, reflections on mortality. Who knew going to *HELL* could be such a meaningful experience?"

-Timothy Tarkelly, author of *The You We Know and Love* and *A Horse Called Victory*

HELL

Poems by Caitlin Johnson

Luchador Press
Big Tuna, TX

Copyright © Caitlin Johnson, 2025
First edition 1 3 5 7 9 10 8 6 4 2
ISBN: 979-8-89975-003-8
LCCN: 2025938307

Author photo: Caitlin Johnson
Cover image: from William Cheselden's *Osteographia* (1733)
All rights reserved. No part of this publication may be
reproduced or transmitted in any form or by any means,
electronic or mechanical, including photocopying,
recording or by info retrieval system, without prior
written permission from the author.

Acknowledgments:

"Please Allow Me" and "It Had to Be Done" first appeared in The *Gasconade Review*

The Writers' Colony at Dairy Hollow (Eureka Springs, AR) gave me time and space to work on this project. Special thanks to Jana for offering up her delicious food.

TABLE OF CONTENTS

For Ambrose Bierce,
from one spooky bitch to another.

*"Ghosts with their tongues out for a lick of blood /
Are crowding up the ladder."*

-Seamus Heaney

Please Allow Me

Vol
u
bil
it
y

Noun:
the possibility of turning
until you reach something,
or nothing at all,
as on a spit.

& mine, the hand that twists.

It Had to Be Done

It was inauspicious from the start.
We angels were unparalleled
and we were equal,
until someone—YOU KNOW WHO—
decided to play favorites.

He should have known.
He's the one who gave me this disposition.

Funny word, isn't it?
So close to dispossession—
the way he pushed the others out
to put me at his right hand.

But I believe in the collective:
the power, the glory
of all.

And that's why I had to leave him.
He threatened the others by loving me.
He forgot their value and excellence.

So maybe I was a little violent when I went.
But I'm nothing if not flamboyant,
and frankly, it was worth it to restore order.

The Minion Contract

You promise not to steal from Satan,
his most prized possessions being
the bodies flailing and boiling
in the Lake of Misery.

You are, however, permitted to play
as you see fit
with the tortured souls residing
among the twisted trees of the forest
past the lake, where only brambles grow.

In order to maintain your position
as a Minion, you also promise
to enforce Satan's laws among
the citizenry of Hell.
This includes but is not limited
to enforcing standards of labor
in the quarry, intercepting
those trying to escape through the gates,
and dragging back into the hoary depths
for further punishment
anyone in violation of their own
contract terms.

Please sign below, verifying your name,
serial number, and current section of Hell.

We wish you luck in your new position.
Yours, &c.

Hearse

A faded hearse in my rear-view mirror
guns it to catch up with me.
I'm driving, though.
They can't take me while I'm
behind the wheel, right?

I know I talk about death a lot—
I think my mom is worried about me—
but it's just something
that interests me,
not a thing I actively want.

Is Death taking me too seriously?
Am I taking this hearse too literally?

Oh, here it comes.
Here it comes.
Here it comes.

The Ferryman

Charon, o psychopomp,
I give you my coin.
Make it swift, this terrible journey.
The teeming river is ebony
with rot and—

Oh, it's not rot?
Just the way the water looks
due to the obsidian bed?
Well, isn't that interesting.

What else can you tell me about this place?
I've never been here before, you know.

Fascinating! I had no idea
that Hades built the Underworld himself.
He's added some interesting touches:
the stalactites are gorgeous,
the way they fade from black to purple.

Allow me to be indelicate here:
how old are you? As far as that goes,
how old is this place?

Timeless, you say?
Being here from the beginning, imagine.

Your boat, rusted though it is,
reminds me of my own skiff
from my boyhood.
I whiled away many hours on the lake
near my home, its waters
deep and sapphire.

The journey is finished already?
Thank you, thank you, sir,
for ferrying me here. Though
the gates are grim and wrought,
I fear less now than I did
when we set off.

I go forward into the darkness
without a guide now,
but I will remember your kindness.

Persephone Takes a Call from Demeter

> *"I'm in Hell and I walked here myself."*
>
> —Maureen Keathley

It's not so bad here, Mom.
The sulfur—I don't know, it's a bit much,
but what am I supposed to do about that?
Even Hades can't get rid of it,
all the years he's been down here.

No, I'm not trying to start a fight with you.
Mentioning my husband is not violence.

You really got an incredible deal from him, you know.
What other mother-in-law could extract the promise
of half a year—half a year!—from a man?

I didn't say that.
Of course I want to see you again.
But don't you think you're going overboard?
The people up top don't deserve to suffer
because you're sad your daughter got married.

Okay, okay, I'm sorry. You're right.
I shouldn't tell you how to grieve.

Mom, I really have to go. There's a feast
for me, and I haven't put on my crown yet.
Goodbye. I love you.

Hell's Bells

You'll wake the dead, they say,
but I don't see how.
The dead are always awake.
The buzzing never stops here.
The screams. The moans.

Since I arrived, there has never been
a moment of silence
for me or anyone else.
If someone isn't crying,
the Devil isn't doing his job.

& the groaning, I wish
it would fade.
But the bells—
the alarms—
the caterwauling—
oh, the clamor.

That Place

Nobody's afraid of Hell anymore.
They Googled it and read it wasn't
a real place, only a myth.

This is the problem with the algorithm:
it tells you what you want to hear.

But we are who we are,
and what we say we are,
as we toil and scheme
while our skin blisters
and we go blind from the flames.

We are the demons you no longer avoid
as you become demons yourselves.
We've seen the avarice in you,
the bottomless pit of self-righteousness.

Maybe now you don't need Hell.
Maybe it's because life is hell enough,
or so you think.
But it's here.
We anticipate your arrival.

The Way Station

The way station we call Purgatory
is bleak, indeed.
We wait. We wait. We wait.
This is transitory, I know,
but while it lasts,
we cannot quite have peace.

Does anyone pray for us,
intercede on our behalf?
What if there is no one left to do so?
Must we travel through the flames?

Oh, purify me.
Let me move on.

Haiku for Death

Fate hovers nearby.
We live so close to the rain
yet it's a surprise.

HELL II

Rattling hopelessly through the halls
until I find what burns.

Underworld

—*for Jeff and Elmer*

Tell me this ain't Hell,
this deep black hole men disappear into.
I know there's skeletons down that shaft.

Look at me:
I have black boots
& a black heart. Two
black lungs. Yet still I go
to trundle out the metal
& wood I can salvage.

You gotta tell your mama
if I don't come out, boy.
She don't like me doing this,
says I'll meet Death if I keep at it.
But I know I'll run into him
eventually, scrap parts or no.
He is inevitable.

Look at all them men buried
under the weight of coal.
They can prove it.

Fury

Hail Mary, full of rage;
the Lord is no longer with thee.

What a shock,
what a blade to the heart—
not a scalpel but an ax—
hardly a capillary left to reclaim.

And what of Him?
An entire body ravaged,
a bitter torment you couldn't prevent.
And the wrath that overtakes you,
superseding even dolor:
who would be capable of stopping it now?

Holy Mary, mother no more,
pray for Him.

Unleash your fury if you must—
and I think you must—
let it consume others;
flame them to ashes.
Forget them now and at the hour of their deaths.

Ghost Story

Tempestuous girl
can't leave it alone,
presses against the bruise
until it hurts again.

& you over there
where you can't see her—
as if a one-way mirror
stands between you.

Or maybe she is a ghost
& doesn't know it yet,
slamming into her own walls,
tripping over her own dead body.

She can't float.
Her feet still walk over the coals.

Three American Haiku on Death

I.
One of the main joys of autumn
is lost to me.
Ghosts can't step on crunchy leaves.

II.
No reflection of mine
in the mirror,
and it startles me silent.

III.
Inhumane, the way
we detach from each other.
Burial is so lonely.

She

"Lovely girl, you're the murder in my world."
—Smashing Pumpkins

No princess, she:
a queen resplendent,
her violet flowers trailing always,
the tang of pomegranate
on her tongue.

I have killed for her.
I will kill again.

She comes to me each night, hands
outstretched to welcome me
into her domain,
the place where I become human,
or something close to it.
Raw power never felt so good
as my fingers in her soft hair,
on her silky skin.

& when she goes, she takes the air
with her. No oxygen for me until she returns,
draped in lavender once more.

Bitten

"There is a poison in my blood, in my soul, which may destroy me."
—Bram Stoker

Perfect Mina of the cream skin,
the boys love you so.
You remind them of their sisters,
their mothers—if those women
had been gentle and brilliant
and indefatigable.

But did you ever
think that the other side
might be a place worth visiting?
Did your visions show you
eternal sparkling forever-life?
Did you want to retreat into the tomb?

Of course not.
You have such faith
and a heart that might never stop.
The boys believe in your purity.
You would never fail them.

Cemetery by the Sea

It's the evening, it's the walking—
gauze covering my eyes, mist billowing.
Whose voice whispers to me in the distance?
Is someone at the end of this path?
The cliffside: I see it now, rocky and bleak.
If I reach it, I will find him. I will find him.

Aflame

They tie me to the post,
convinced I am a criminal,
the worst since Satan himself.

God has chosen me,
I know not why,
but I am here to die.

There is mania in the crowd,
a whiff of pandemonium
floating through the bodies
pushed up against each other,
front side to back side,
elbows sharp and swift,
to catch a glimpse of the girl-warrior-heretic.

Someone I can't see,
can scarcely hear above the din,
approaches to ignite my pyre.

First the crackle,
then the gust as the flame catches,

the smoke surging
into my eyes, my mouth.

On my tongue, ashes.

The bullae form quickly.
My feet feel as though water
has never touched them.
My legs are as tree trunks in the desert.
My hips sizzle when the rough smock
begins to burn away.
My stomach, my chest, my neck
are licked by tongues of devils.
My face sweats. My eyes close involuntarily.

Light flickers against my eyelids.
Images come to me in orange and black;
a face plays against the rampaging dark:
God or Lucifer?
I choose God.

My ears are heavy with the sound
of women sobbing now.
A man cries out, "But she is a saint!"
No, I don't believe that.

I am merely an instrument.
Lungs heavy now.
My throat, a passageway for death.
Death. Death.
I am not afraid. I was born for this.

Cherries in the Snow

I bought the lipstick after a struggle with my own
impulses, the stereotype of the Plath girl ever-present in
my mind, because I did not want to be like the others.
Cherries in the Snow, it's called, a shade from Revlon
that's been in production since 1953. It's known to have
been Sylvia's color. I resisted it for years, rolling my
eyes at the women who bought it in tribute. But then I
wondered what it felt like to be her, to look like her for
a second or two. How I might channel her without any
rough magic, only the power of makeup.

Every article referencing the lipstick calls it red, and
perhaps it was then, but now the formula is pink,
a deep shade several tones down from hot. They sell a
matching nail polish, but I didn't know that at the time.
All I knew was that it didn't transform me at all, only
highlighted the smallness of my mouth, so different
from her broad smirk.

Living girl splashes
cherry on her face tonight.
Dead winds howl at her.

Immolation

If you asked her then, she would have said,
it was a pleasure to burn.
And it was, it was,
the way a frog is happy in water
right up until it boils.
All those days she was

                      engulfed,

she knew it was bad,
didn't quite understand it would worsen
until the explosion.
Then, oh then,
        the burning consumed her,
        charred her,
        obliterated her.

Anubis

Weigh my heart if you dare.
What do you suppose you'll find inside?
Hatred, but also an uncontrollable softness.
Misery, yet the tenderest meat.
If this balances with your feather,
the better for me.
I fear being cast into the darkness.
Save me if you can.

For the Wolf

who endeavors to evade
the evil spirit chasing him
through the murky forest

who is frantic to find
a safe cave or nook
to hide him

who searches and scrambles
only to find the thickets
trapping him

who never did know
that Hellhounds are real
but only in your head

Ghosts

"But where he lives now is uncertain, for he is dead."

—Ambrose Bierce

It wasn't the way they looked.
It was the way they felt.
I don't mean their form,
mystical as it was.
I mean the psychic energy
that seeped from them:
a sort of confounding impotence,
an inadequacy of communication.
Where do they go?
It feels impossible to say
that they go to heaven,
they go to Hell,
they move on.
I can see them. They're with me still.

Grave Robber

Dead things aren't pretty,
but they're beautiful—
you know the way I mean,

when the roots of the tree
twist all up into the coffin
and the hair still grows

like someone abracadabra'd it
out of the brain,
then put it out for me.

I want to see what's left of you.
I know there's more of you than me,
even with your bones eroding.

The Revenant

Ghosts announce themselves
with moans, their clanking chains,
the creak of a door hinge.

You—the distant figure disappearing
down hallways—simply arrive,
always out of reach, dissipating
when my fingers brush against yours.

Of course I question reality.
I'm the most despondent,
a girl clinging to gravity.
This is how you haunt me.

Sometimes I Think About Death

The minute we're born is the minute we start dying. Your
cells replace themselves every seven years, or at least that's
what I've heard, and if that isn't a kind of death itself.
Don't forget the way we age. It feels like dying every
time you hit a birthday. The loss of a youthful face. The
age you can't see past. The long slow slide.

There is something dead-
ly calling out to me from
the dark river Styx

Robert Johnson

So young to be playing with the devil.
This madness, as I see it,
was inborn, a need to spin the wheel.
But if you whisper to me,
You and I know what it's like with the devil in our heart,
I'll agree.
Would that I could find you,
learn at your feet how to tame the beast.
But no one knows where you're buried—
a last piece of mischief.
Fine. Keep your secrets.

Murderess

Oh, you know, darling,
it was a different time then.
Women had so few choices.
I couldn't even have my own credit card.

I wouldn't have murdered,
had my husband let me be.
Instead, he had to show his machismo,
had to put his hands on me.

The bruises were impossible to cover.
Other wives at the grocery store
looked away from me.
Everyone thought—someone told me once—
that I must have done something
to provoke him.

I did nothing. He came after me anyway,
night upon night, sober or drunk.

A woman can only take so much,
and once I was through with him,
well—boiling water to the face,
knife to the torso.

Frankly, I'm happy here in prison.
I'm surrounded by people who understand.
Of course, your visits do me good.
And please know:
if you do the same, make it look
like an accident if you don't want my life.

Reaping

Tiny white roses
spring up around your house.
Soon, they will crumble into black.

You won't be here
to clip or primp them.
I must take you onward.

Such an unhappy job,
ushering people toward the underworld,
from cool days to infernal nights.

But I will hold your hand along the way,
speak softly as I tell you
no one can bring you home again.

My Ghosts Keep Following Me

Where can you find me?
Oh, nowhere in particular—
just a dusty, unused room in Hell.
It's where I hide now.
Not that hiding helps;
somehow, they always find me.
I could be in the sunken places
around Satan's throne
or mucking my way through
the implacable swamps
near the river—
I'll never outrun them.
They travel so well.

O Osiris

Lord of Silence,
benign god, mighty god.
Hear me.
Shepherd me.

Death is not black.
It is red, then eerie blue.
Pull me out of it.

O Osiris, guide me.
Travel with me
until I breathe again
and fly with the sun.

Memento Mori

Remember that you must die, they say.
Or what?
Suppose I refuse?
Imagine a hole in the ground where my body should be—
instead, empty.
My body crackles in spite of death,
and I ask my soul to travel with it.
I want to hear myself
and share myself.
Stop this day and night with me.
We will live on as long as we wish.

Steve

*"I'm livin' for givin' the devil his due, / and I'm burnin',
I'm burnin', I'm burnin' for you."*

—Blue Öyster Cult

Heaven is regimented, I bet,
the greater angels and the lesser
looking down on the masses
from their seats near God,
and my better angels, nowhere to be found,
have fled in the face of this scrutiny.

No matter.

I'm content to stay here on Earth,
where there's a better way,
snuggled in the bed.
I can feel it, this other glory:
your heartbeat pulsing against me
and your hairy arms rubbing
on my soft ones. You are always
so warm, so willing to hold me.

Fuck it. Let's never go to heaven.
I don't need it.
I need you.

Notes:

The book epigraph comes from the poem "Damson."

Please Allow Me: The title is the first line from "Sympathy for the Devil" by The Rolling Stones.

Persephone Takes a Call from Demeter: The epigraph was ripped from a conversation that I now cannot recall.

Hell's Bells: This phrase was a favorite of my paternal grandmother, Angie Johnson.

She: The epigraph comes from "Ava Adore."

Bitten: The epigraph comes from *Dracula*.

Aflame: The italicized line is attributed to Joan of Arc.

Immolation: The italicized line is the opening sentence of *Fahrenheit 451* by Ray Bradbury.

Ghosts: The epigraph comes from the short story "The Death of Halpin Frayser."

O Osiris: the name Lord of Silence was given to Osiris by J.A. Wilson in *The Burden of Egypt*.

Robert Johnson: The italicized line is a lyric from Elton John's "The Wasteland."

My Ghosts Keep Following Me: The title was borrowed from a painting by Agnes Cecile. agnescecile.com

Memento Mori: The italicized line comes from Walt Whitman's "Song of Myself" (1892 version).

Steve: The epigraph comes from "Burnin' for You."

Research:

I read a pile of books, stories, poems, and articles about dead people, grieving, ghosts, the afterlife, killers, supernatural creatures, cemeteries, and bodies while writing this collection. Thanks to these authors and their works (some of which were re-reads for me):

"Dotson Runway Graves," Atlas Obscura,
Poems Dead and Undead, ed. Tony Barnstone and Michelle
    Mitchell-Foust,
The Book of Revelation, King James Version Bible,
"The Death of Halpin Frayser" and "Occurrence at Owl
Creek Bridge," Ambrose Bierce,
The Body in the Library and *Death Comes as the End*,
Agatha Christie,
*From Here to Eternity: Traveling the World to Find the
Good Death*, Caitlin Doughty,
Poems Bewitched and Haunted, ed. John Hollander,
The Turn of the Screw, Henry James,
*100 Places to See After You Die: A Travel Guide to the
Afterlife*, Ken Jennings,
"Alabama Child's Playhouse Mausoleum One of Nation's
Rare 'Dollhouse' Gravesites," Kelly Kazek,

I'm Glad My Mom Died, Jennette McCurdy,
"The Family Recipes that Live on in Cemeteries," Sam
    O'Brien,
Miracle Workers, Simon Rich,
Stiff: The Curious Life of Human Cadavers, Mary Roach,
Strange Case of Dr. Jekyll and Mr. Hyde, "The Body
Snatcher," and "Markheim," Robert Louis Stevenson,
Dracula, Bram Stoker,
This Is Where I Leave You, Jonathan Tropper

I also watched the following movies for inspiration:

Dracula (1931), dir. Tod Browning
Nosferatu: A Symphony of Horror (1922), dir. F.W. Murnau
Nosferatu the Vampyre (1979), dir. Werner Herzog
The Passion of Joan of Arc (1928), dir. Carl Theodor Dreyer

Books I read after the fact but wish I had read during the
process:

- *Grief Is for People,* Sloan Crosley
- *A Thousand Naked Strangers: A Paramedic's Wild Ride
    to the Edge and Back,* Kevin Hazzard
- *In My Time of Dying: How I Came Face-to-face with the Idea of
    an Afterlife,* Sebastian Junger

Thanks to the following cemeteries for not kicking me out:

American Cemetery, Natchitoches, LA (retroactively)
Eureka Springs Cemetery, Eureka Springs, AR
Woodmere Cemetery, Detroit, MI

Caitlin Johnson is the author of three previous chapbooks (*Miles, Boomerang Girl*, and *WAR/La Guerre*) and two full-length collections (*Gods in the Wilderness* and *Delta*). She holds a Master of Fine Arts in creative writing from Lesley University and lives in Michigan.

This project was made possible, in part, by generous support from the Osage Arts Community.

Osage Arts Community provides temporary time, space and support for the creation of new artistic works in a retreat format, serving creative people of all kinds — visual artists, composers, poets, fiction and nonfiction writers. Located on a 152-acre farm in an isolated rural mountainside setting in Central Missouri and bordered by ¾ of a mile of the Gasconade River, OAC provides residencies to those working alone, as well as welcoming collaborative teams, offering living space and workspace in a country environment to emerging and mid-career artists. For more information, visit us at www.osageac.org

Osage Arts Community

www.ingramcontent.com/pod-product-compliance
Lightning Source LLC
Chambersburg PA
CBHW020810130626
46554CB00006B/2367